TITLE II-A

KATE GREENAWAY'S

BOOK OF GAMES

PUSS IN THE CORNER.

THE child who represents puss stands in the middle, while the others stand at fixed stations round her. One then beckons to another saying: "Puss, puss, give me a drop of water!" when each runs and change places. Puss then runs

and tries to get into one of the places, if she succeeds, the one left out is puss.

KATE GREENAWAY'S
BOOK OF GAMES

A STUDIO BOOK
THE VIKING PRESS · NEW YORK

Published in 1976 by
The Viking Press
625 Madison Avenue, New York, N.Y. 10022

Published simultaneously in Canada by
The Macmillan Company of Canada Limited

Library of Congress catalog card number: 76-000331

SBN 670-41184-1

Printed in Holland by
THE YSEL PRESS, DEVENTER
Bound in Great Britain by
WEBB SON & CO. LTD., FERNDALE
Produced by
ASH & GRANT LTD.,
120B PENTONVILLE ROAD, LONDON N1 9JB

CONTENTS.

CONTENTS—*continued.*

LIST OF ILLUSTRATIONS.

KATE GREENAWAY'S

BOOK OF GAMES

•••••••••••••••••••••••••••••

I LOVE MY LOVE WITH AN "A."

ONE player says : "I love my love with an 'A,' because she is
AMIABLE ; I hate her with an 'A,' because she is ARTFUL. Her
name is ALICE, she comes from AMERICA and I gave her an APPLE."
The next player says : " I love my love with a 'B,' because she is
BEAUTIFUL ; I hate her with a 'B,' because she is BOASTFUL. Her
name is BERTHA, she comes from BIRMINGHAM and I gave her a
BRACELET." The next player takes " C "; and the next " D "; and so
on through all the letters in the alphabet.

(II)

TEA - POT.

ONE player leaves the room, while the others decide on a word with many meanings. The absent player having been called in, his object is to find out the chosen word. To enable him to do this, the others converse about it, but instead of using the word itself, say "tea-pot" instead. For instance, if the word chosen be "rain," the players converse about it in the following manner :—"We shall have 'tea-pot' (rain) to-night. When I was riding yesterday, the 'tea-pot' (rein) broke. The 'tea-pot' (reign) of Queen Victoria has been long and glorious." When the player correctly guesses the hidden word, the person whose remark enabled him to do so, leaves the room in his turn.

THE CHRISTMAS BAG.

FILL a large paper bag with sweets, biscuits, or small toys, and tie a piece of string round the top to prevent the things falling out. Then suspend the bag from the door frame. Blindfold the children in succession, beginning from the youngest upwards, and give them a stick with which they must try to hit the bag. Each child is allowed three trials. When a hole is made in the bag, and its contents scattered on the floor, the children scramble for them.

TOPS.

TOPS are common enough objects to most people, but there is some skill required in spinning them. There are also many different games. For "Peg in the Ring" (played with a peg top), draw a circle about three feet in diameter. One player begins by throwing his top into the centre, and whilst it is spinning the other players peg their tops at it, but if it gets out of the ring, and ceases spinning, the owner may pick it up and peg it at any others spinning in the circle. To set whipping tops going, they should be rapidly twirled round with the hands, and whipped, not too hardly at first. An eel skin makes the best kind of whip. Races can be played with whip tops, the boy who can whip his top along at the greatest speed is the winner. Another game called "Encounters" consists in the players whipping their tops against each other till one of them falls.

THE SHEPHERDESS AND THE WOLF.

THE players stand in a row at one end of the lawn while the shepherdess stands at the other. Half-way between the wolf must be concealed behind a bush. The shepherdess then calls out: "Sheep, sheep, come home!" One of the sheep replies: "I'm afraid of the wolf!" The shepherdess then says: "The wolf has gone to Devonshire and won't be home for seven years; sheep, sheep, come home!" The sheep then singly try to reach the shepherdess without being caught by the wolf. And so the game continues till all the players have either been caught by the wolf or reached the shepherdess safely.

THE STORY GAME.

ONE of the players starts an original story, and leaves off in a very exciting place; his left-hand neighbour must instantly continue it, and also stops at an exciting point; when the thread of the story is resumed by the player on his left hand. For example, one player starts the following story: "One evening, several centuries ago, a knight was riding through a dark wood, when hearing a noise he looked up and saw——" Here the player stops, and his left-hand neighbour continues: "A band of robbers rapidly advancing towards him. He gave himself up for lost, when——" The story is continued by his left-hand neighbour, and so the game goes on till the tale is finished by the last player.

TIRZA, OR DOUBLE TAGG.

THE players stand in pairs one behind another in the form of a circle facing the centre. There must be two odd players, one of whom runs away while the other catches. Directly the player who is being pursued places himself in front of any couple he is safe, while the hindermost person of the trio becomes the pursued. If he is caught before placing himself in front of another couple, he becomes pursuer.

WHAT IS MY THOUGHT LIKE?

ONE player thinks of some person or object and then asks each of the others in turn: "What is my thought like?" Each names some object and the leader then announces what his thought was; and each player is requested to prove the resemblance between his guess and the subject really chosen. If he cannot he must pay a forfeit.

PROHIBITIONS

THE players decide to dress a lady, but the following colours—GREEN, YELLOW, BLUE, and PINK must not be used. One player asks of each in turn: "How will you dress my lady?" One says: "In a white silk dress!" Another: "With a wreath on her head!" and so on. Whoever mentions the forbidden colours pays a forfeit.

TWENTY QUESTIONS.

ONE of the players is sent out of the room, and the others agree upon some subject, which he is to discover by asking twenty questions; and they must all be of such a nature as can be answered by "Yes" or "No."

SEE-SAW.

A GREAT deal of amusement may be derived from having a see-saw. It should be made of a thick plank of wood balanced over a fallen tree-trunk or other suitable erection. The players sit on the ends, balancing themselves as equally as possible, and go up and down. If one player will stand in the middle to work it, he can help to balance it and prevent a sudden jerk should anyone fall or get off without warning.

THE RHYMING DUMB CRAMBO.

ONE player thinks of a noun and gives the others a word that rhymes with it, and they must ask him questions about it in verse. For instance, suppose "hat" to be the word thought of, and "bat" that given to the players, as rhyming with it, one asks —

> "Is it the animal on the rug,
> That lies curled up so very snug?"

The one who has set the word answers "No, it is not 'cat.'" Then another of the party gives a rhyming guess.

EARTH, AIR, FIRE, AND WATER.

THE players form a circle, and one stands in the centre holding a handkerchief knotted into a ball. He counts up to ten, then throws the ball into someone's lap, calling out either "Earth," "Air," "Fire," or "Water." If he cries "Earth," the person in whose lap the handkerchief has fallen must instantly name some animal which lives on the earth; if the word was "Water," some fish must be named; if "Fire," something that can exist in fire; if "Air," some bird. If he allows the ball-thrower to count up to ten without his answering he must pay a forfeit.

(18)

MARBLES.

MANY and various are the games which can be played with marbles. "Ring-taw" is a very favourite pastime. Two circles are drawn on the ground, the outer one six feet in diameter, the inner one nine inches. The players put one or more marbles inside the inner circle, and shoot one at a time from the outer ring at them. As long as a player does not send a marble out of the ring he may shoot indefinitely. When they have all fired once, they shoot from the place where their marbles remained, not the original starting place. If a player drives a marble out of the circle he wins it and shoots again, but if his "taw" remains in he is out, and must put a marble in the circle. There are other games called "Conqueror," "Increase Pound," "Three Holes," "Lag Out," and "Snops and Spans."

THE FEATHER GAME.

THE players sit close together, and one of them taking a piece of swansdown (or similar substance), blows it up into the air. The other players must keep it afloat by their breath, if anyone allows it to sink to the ground he must pay a forfeit.

JINGLERS.

ALL the players but one are blindfolded. He moves about the room ringing a bell; while the others, guided by the sound, endeavour to catch him. The player that succeeds in doing so takes his place.

TOUCH WOOD.

ALL the children but one place
themselves in various positions, each
touching something that is wood.
They keep constantly running from
one wooden thing to another. The
one left out runs after them, and
the first she catches not touching
wood takes her place.

I HAVE A BASKET.

ONE player remarks: "I have a basket!" The others ask: "What have you in it?" He mentions some article beginning with "A." The next player then says: "I have a basket!" The others repeat their question, and he replies by mentioning something beginning with "B;" and so the game continues through all the letters in the alphabet.

HUNT THE RING.

A RING is threaded on a long piece of string with the ends joined. The players stand in a circle, the cord passing through their closed hands. The ring circulates from one to another, while a player in the centre of the circle endeavours to find it; when he does so, the person in whose hand the ring is found takes his place.

DROP THE HANDKERCHIEF.

THE players stand in a circle and join hands. One walks round outside the ring and drops a handkerchief behind one of the players, who instantly picks it up and pursues him. When he catches him the two change places and the game goes on as before.

BATTLEDORE & SHUTTLECOCK.

THIS is a most convenient game, because one
solitary individual can find amusement
as well as any number, provided there
is a bat for each player. The object
of the game is to keep the
shuttlecock going as long
as possible.

THE DRAWING GAME.

THE players must all be provided with paper and pencils, and each makes a rough sketch at the top of his paper, illustrating some historical or well known scene. Writing at the bottom what it is, and turning over what he has written, he passes the drawing on to the player on his left hand, who writes at the bottom what he thinks it represents, then turning over what he has written, he passes the drawing on to his left-hand neighbour ; and so the game continues till all the sketches have been passed round the table, when each player reads out the various suggestions as to what his own drawing represents.

SPINNING THE TRENCHER.

THE players sit in a circle and each takes the name of some flower ; one then moves to the centre of the circle and sets a trencher or plate spinning on the floor ; then he runs back to his seat crying " Honeysuckle " or any other flower that has been chosen by the players. " Honeysuckle " rushes forward to prevent the trencher stopping, then returns to his seat, after spinning the trencher again and calling out some other name. Any player who, when called, allows the trencher to fall, must pay a forfeit.

HOW, WHEN, AND WHERE.

THE players sit in a line. One who is chosen to ask the questions goes out of the room. The players then choose a word with many meanings. When they have fixed on it the person outside is called in and goes down the line of players saying to each: "How do you like it?" Then he walks down a second time asking: "When do you like it?" Then a third time saying: "Where do you like it?" From the answers he guesses what the word is.

UP JENKINS.

THE company divide into two parties and sit round a table. One party then puts their hands under the table and a shilling or other small article is placed in one of the palms. The other side then calls out: "Up Jenkins!" and the players whose side has the shilling concealed must all place their closed hands on the table. The opposite side must then guess in which hand the shilling is concealed. The hands that they think have not got it must be told to go down, but if one of those hands should contain it, the player must show it, and the same side hides the shilling again. But if all the hands but one are sent down without the shilling being found, then the player must give it up, and the opposite side hides it in the same manner.

HUNT THE SLIPPER.

THE children sit on the ground, or on low seats in a circle, with their knees raised.   One has been left out ; she brings a slipper, and giving it to one child says :—

"COBBLER, cobbler, mend my shoe,
Get it done by half-past two."

She goes away, and comes back in about a minute and asks if it is done.   (During this time the slipper has been passing round.)   The child answers, she thinks her neighbour has it; so the seeker passes on to her, and getting the same answer she has to go round till the slipper is found. If she is a long time finding it, the slipper may be thrown across the circle.

MUSICAL CHAIRS.

SOMEONE plays the piano. Chairs must be placed down the room, back to back, one less in number than the players who galop round them in time to the music. Suddenly it stops, and everybody then tries to get a chair, but as there is one short someone will be left standing, and is then out of the game. A chair is taken away and the game goes on as before till only one player, the victor, is left.

KING OF THE CASTLE.

ONE player ascends a little hillock and calls himself " King of the Castle ;" the others immediately try to pull or push him off, while he strives to the utmost to repel them and retain his position. The player who succeeds in deposing him, becomes " King of the Castle " in his place.

MULBERRY BUSH.

THE children form into a ring, and holding hands run round and sing :—

> " HERE we go round the mulberry bush,
>   The mulberry bush, the mulberry bush ;
>   Here we go round the mulberry bush
>   On a cold and frosty morning."

Then unloosening hands they pretend to wash them, and say :—

> "THIS is the way we wash our hands,
> Wash our hands, wash our hands ;
> This is the way we wash our hands
> On a cold and frosty morning."

They then go round in ring again and sing " mulberry bush," to be again followed by pretending to wash faces, dresses, go to school, and anything they like.

FOX AND HEN.

ONE of the players is chosen to be fox and another to be hen. All the others are chickens, and form a string at the back of the hen one behind another. They then advance to the fox's den and ask him the time. They repeat the question several times till he says it is twelve o'clock at night, when they must instantly run away as the fox will pursue them, the hen dodging the fox and trying to prevent his seizing the last chicken. When all the chickens have been captured the game is finished.

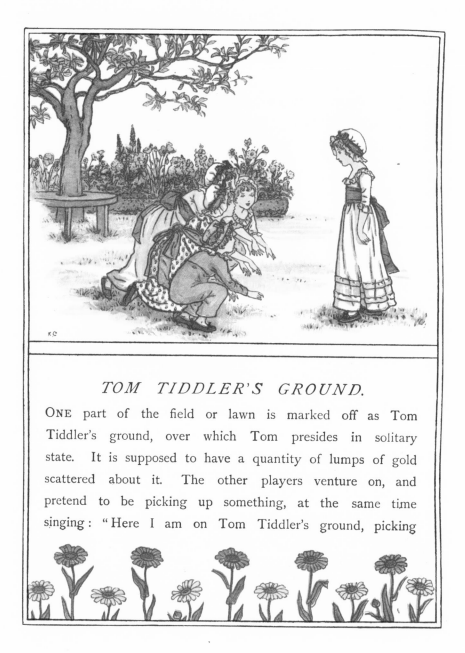

TOM TIDDLER'S GROUND.

ONE part of the field or lawn is marked off as Tom
Tiddler's ground, over which Tom presides in solitary
state. It is supposed to have a quantity of lumps of gold
scattered about it. The other players venture on, and
pretend to be picking up something, at the same time
singing: "Here I am on Tom Tiddler's ground, picking

up gold and silver!" He rushes after them, and if he succeeds in catching anybody, that one has to take his place as Tom Tiddler. Tom may not leave his own ground.

WORDS AND QUESTIONS.

EACH player writes on separate pieces of paper a question and a noun. The papers are then shuffled, and each player draws out a question and a noun; the former he must answer in rhyme, and bring the latter into his answer. Then one player reads aloud all the questions and answers.

PROVERBS.

ONE of the party is sent out of the room while the others choose a proverb. When one is selected each person in turn takes a word of the proverb which he must bring into his answer when questioned by the absent player, who asks a question of each in turn, and from their answers guesses the proverb.

HOP SCOTCH.

CHALK out on the ground a figure like the accompanying diagram. Then the players "pink;" that is, throw their piece of tile, or lead, towards the pudding, or top of the figure. The one who lodges his tile there begins; if more than one succeeds in doing this, they "pink" again. The winner begins by standing at *, and throwing his tile into the division marked 1 ; he then hops into the space and kicks the tile out to the starting point. Then he throws the tile into 2; hops into 1, then into 2, and kicks the tile out as before. He repeats this through the different numbers till he arrives at 8; here he may put his feet into 6 and 7 and rest himself, but he must begin hopping again before he kicks the tile home. He then goes on through 9, 10, 11, as before directed. 12 is another resting-place, where he may put down both feet. When he comes to plum pudding he must kick the tile with such force that it goes through all the other beds by one kick. In the other divisions it is not necessary to kick the tile so hard, as the player may hop as many times as he likes. If he throws the tile into a wrong number, or if it rests on a line, he loses his innings, whether kicking it out or throwing it in to begin with. He also misses his turn if he puts his feet down in what is not a resting-place, or if he puts his feet on a line, or kicks the tile outside the diagram.

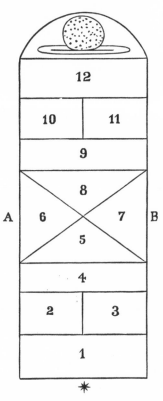

ORANGES AND LEMONS.

THE two tallest players, taking the name of orange and lemon respectively, join hands, and holding them up form an arch under which the others pass in single file, holding on to each others' dresses, singing :—

"ORANGES and lemons," say the bells of St. Clements.
" Brickbats and tiles," say the bells of St. Giles.

"You owe me five farthings," say the bells of St. Martin's.
"When will you pay me?" say the bells of Old Bailey.
"When I grow rich," say the bells of Shoreditch.
"When will that be?" say the bells of Stepney.
"I do not know," says the great bell of Bow.
Here comes a candle to light you to bed,
And here comes a chopper to chop off your head!

When the last one comes below the arms they descend and catch him, and he is asked in a whisper if he will be orange or lemon. He whispers the answer and joins whichever he has chosen holding on round her waist. The game continues thus till all are caught, when a tug-of-war ensues between the two parties.

DUMB CRAMBO.

HALF the party leave the room and the rest choose a word which the others are to guess and act. They then tell those outside that the word they have chosen rhymes with "die," or any other word selected. The players enter the room and act in dumb show one of the words that rhyme with "die." If it is wrong, the audience hiss; if right, they clap and go out of the room in their turn.

HOOPS.

EVERY child knows, or ought to know, the pleasure of bowling a hoop. What a nice ring there is about it, when on a fine frosty day the juvenile members of the family all turn out with hoops and race along the road. There is a very jolly game called "turnpikes," but it wants rather an open space; any number can play, only half the players need hoops. Two largish stones or bricks are placed side by side about six inches apart at regular intervals in a circle or along a road, each pair being guarded by a "pike-keeper." The bowlers, who all stand in a row, start at some little distance off and drive their hoops between the bricks. If they succeed in doing this, they steer round and go through again; but should anyone miss, he takes the place of "pike-keeper" whose gate he missed, and the "pike-keeper" becomes a bowler.

THE ANGLER AND THE FISH.

THE players each take the name of a fish; one is blindfolded and stands in the middle of the room singing: "Little fish that come out of the sea, eat the fly that here you see," and he throws out a long string attached to which is an imaginary bait. One of the players, all of whom have in the meantime been moving round the fisher, seizes the line. The fisher has then to guess which fish pulls; if he guesses wrongly, the fish drops the line and they move round as before; if rightly, he must describe his fish-nature, and is then blindfolded in his turn, while the late angler joins the moving players.

FROG IN THE MIDDLE.

THE child who represents the frog sits on a hassock in the
middle of the room, all the other children
run and dance round, singing :—

"FROG in the middle, you can't catch me !
Frog in the middle, you can't catch me !"

FROG IN THE MIDDLE—*continued*.

"Frog" must try to catch them with her hands without getting up from her stool; the one who is caught has to take the place of "Frog."

RUSSIAN SCANDAL.

THE players sit in a circle and the leader whispers some anecdote or quotation to his left-hand neighbour, which he in turn repeats to the person next him, and so the story is whispered round the circle, the last player relating aloud what has been told him. The original is then repeated, and it is amusing to see how entirely different the two narratives are.

THE ADJECTIVE GAME.

ONE of the players leaves the room, while the others agree on an adjective which the absent player has to discover by questioning the others in turn. They must answer the questions in such a manner as will illustrate the adjective they have chosen. For instance, if they have fixed upon "abruptly," each player must answer the question put to him in an abrupt manner.

SWINGS.

A SWING is a source of much innocent
enjoyment which most children can have
for a very small outlay. It consists of two
upright posts, with a bar securely fastened
horizontally; to this two ropes are tied to
which a seat is attached. A bough of a tree
is a more picturesque place for a swing,
but trees are not always to be had for
the wishing. Boat swings at fairs are
irresistible attractions to most boys.

HIDE-AND-SEEK.

ONE child called "he" must hide his
eyes at a spot called "home." While the
other children run away and hide. When they
are hidden, they call *whoop!* Then "he" uncovering
his eyes, runs out and tries to catch them before they can
get "home." The one caught is "he" next time. If
none are caught, then the same one must be "he" again.

MAGIC MUSIC.

THE company sit in a circle, and one person is sent out of the room. Then the players either hide or alter something in the room or agree that the absent one shall do something, such as repeat a verse of poetry, etc. When they have decided the player is called in, and may ask whether it is something to find, alter, or do. He is told which it is, and someone must then begin playing on the piano. When he is near finding, altering, or doing, the thing decreed, the music is loud; but when he moves away from the thing hidden or altered, or does not guess what he has to do, the music is soft. It is by listening to its sound, that the player is guided in performing his task.

THE STOOL OF REPENTANCE.

ONE of the players leaves the room, while the others each write on slips of paper their opinion of him. For instance, one writes: "He is very conceited!" Another: "Extremely good-natured!" and so on. The person outside is then summoned, and one of the players reads out the various opinions of him. As he does so, the player must guess whose opinion it is, when he does so correctly, that person goes out of the room in his turn.

BLIND MAN'S BUFF.

ONE child has her eyes blindfolded with a handkerchief, so that she cannot see, and is placed in the middle of the room. The Children say to her: "How many horses has your father got?" She replies: "Three!" Children: "What colours are they?" She: "Black, White, and Grey!" Children: "Turn round three times and catch who you may!" Then then turn her round three times, and she tries to catch anyone she can; the one caught has to be next "blind man."

THROWING THE HANDKERCHIEF.

THE players sit in a circle and one stands up in the centre. A handkerchief twisted into a ball is then thrown from one side to another, and the person in the middle must try and catch it. When he succeeds in doing so, he takes the place of the player who last threw the handkerchief, and who in his turn enters the circle to try and catch it.

CLUMPS.

THE players sit in two circles as far from each other as possible. One person from each leaves the room and they then agree upon some subject, such as "Little Red Riding Hood," which the others must try and find out. They each go to the other's circle, sit in the middle, and are questioned by the players whose object it is to be the first to discover the person or thing thought of.

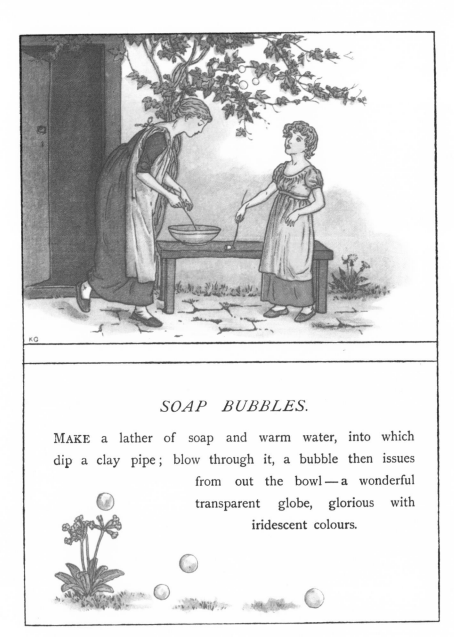

SOAP BUBBLES.

MAKE a lather of soap and warm water, into which
dip a clay pipe; blow through it, a bubble then issues
from out the bowl — a wonderful
transparent globe, glorious with
iridescent colours.

SCHOOLMISTRESS.

ONE of the players, chosen to be schoolmistress, sits facing the rest and says: "I have thought of some place (or substance) beginning with 'G.'" Each in turn must suggest a place or substance beginning with "G," before the schoolmistress can count up to ten. Whoever guesses the right place or thing goes to the top of the class.

THE HIDDEN WORD.

ONE of the players leaves the room, while the others agree on a word. The absent player is then called in, and asks questions in turn of the others, who must all bring into their answers the word previously agreed upon. By this means, the hidden word is guessed.

THE OLD SOLDIER.

THE players sit in a circle whilst one walks round saying: "Here comes an old soldier from Botany Bay, and what have you got to give him to day?" In answering him, the following words must not be used—WHITE, BLACK, or GREY; YES, NO, or NAY. If they are a forfeit must be paid.

FOLLOW-MY-LEADER.

AN active and daring boy should be chosen as leader, the others follow him one behind the other, as closely as they can, doing as he does, and going where he goes, over gates, stiles, and obstacles of all kinds. If anyone fails in accomplishing any one feat, he takes his place behind the rest. The next one who fails goes behind him, and so the game continues until the leader chooses to stop.

JUDGE AND JURY.

THE players are arranged in two rows facing each other, the judge sits at the end, he asks one of the jury a question. The game is that the one questioned must not answer, but his opposite companion replies for him, the answer need not be to the point but must not contain the words—YES or NO; BLACK or WHITE. Anyone answering out of turn or after the judge has counted ten, becomes questioner in his turn.

THE HAT GAME.

A HAT is placed on the ground, and the players (standing two or three paces from it) try to throw cards, one at a time, into it. This sounds much more easy to do than it really is.

DRAWING GAME.

ONE person draws the head of a person, animal, bird or anything else, and folds it over, leaving a mark where the neck comes. The next player draws a body and folding it over passes it to a third, who draws legs. As no one knows what the one before has drawn, the results cause great amusement.

FRENCH AND ENGLISH.

THE players divide into two parties standing opposite to each other. One side has a red and the other a white flag, lightly fixed in the ground. It is the object of each side to obtain possession of the other's flag. If anyone is caught in the attempt, he is taken prisoner, and must be rescued by his companions before the flag can be seized.

BLOWING OUT THE CANDLE.

A PERSON is blindfolded and turned round two or three times, and is then told to blow the candle out : he generally manages to blow very wide of the mark.

BOOK CONSEQUENCES.

ALL the players being furnished with paper and pencil, the title of a book is written on the top edge of the paper and folded down. It is then passed on to the next person, who writes an alternative title, and passes it to a third, who writes an author's name. The fourth writes the subject of the book, a fifth player an extract from it, and a sixth a criticism. After each person has written, he folds the paper over and passes it on.

POINTER'S BUFF.

ONE player is blindfolded, and a stick is placed in his hand. The others then dance in a circle round him, till he points his stick at one of the players who immediately takes hold of it. The blindfolded person then asks him a question which he must answer in a disguised voice. The " blindman " then guesses who it is If he guesses correctly, that player takes his place; but if not, the circle dances round as before till another player is pointed at.

THROWING LIGHT.

TWO of the players privately agree upon a word with many meanings. They then converse about it to each other making such remarks as will throw light on the word. In the meantime the rest of the players are endeavouring to guess what it is. When anyone thinks he has discovered the word, he makes such a remark as will show the initiated that he has guessed it. He must then whisper to them what word he thinks it is; if he is wrong, his handkerchief is thrown over his face till he successfully guesses what the word is, but if he has guessed the word correctly, he joins with the two players in "throwing light" upon it. The game continues till everyone has guessed the word.

KITES.

MOST boys and girls know how to make and fly a kite. On a fine windy day, what can be more delightful than a good run over a common or breezy hill. Even a wet day need not come amiss, it gives a good opportunity for mending them or for making new ones. Japanese kites made in the shape of birds are amusing novelties and look very imposing. Paper " messengers " of all descriptions may be sent up the string ; as they speed up, turning rapidly round and round, they can be followed by the eye till they reach the kite. Parachutes are also easily made, but as no string is attached, they are not so readily captured again.

WHO'LL TAKE THE CHAIR?

THE players form a circle and one stands up in the centre and tries to obtain a seat, while the others rapidly slip from one chair to another. When he finds an empty chair, he takes possession of it, and the person who allowed him to do so must try in his turn to get a seat in the same manner.

THE KNIGHT OF THE WHISTLE.

THE players sit in a circle, and one who does not know the game goes into the centre to hunt the whistle. The others fasten it to her dress and blow it behind her, but keep their hands in motion all the time as if they were passing it. Of course the whistle must always be blown so that she does not see it.

DOLLS.

MOST little girls like to possess a
large family of dolls, though they
may vary more in size and shape
than an ancient Egyptian and a nineteenth
century Masher. There are the tiny little
dolls which lie in uncomfortable attitudes
in dolls' houses decked out in bright

colours. There is the Dutch doll, with its stiffly-jointed legs and arms. There is the heavy old-fashioned wooden doll, as large as a good-sized baby. And now we have dolls which open and shut their eyes and say "Papa!" "Mamma!" Anyone who wishes to become a good needlewoman should try making dolls' clothes, where neat work is essential to the look of the thing.

HIDING THE THIMBLE.

THE players are sent out of the room while someone hides a thimble in a place where it can be seen. The players are then called in, and as each one discovers the thimble, he sits down in silence. The person who first sees it, hides it next time.

SHOUTING PROVERBS.

ONE player leaves the room and the others choose a proverb, of which they each take a word. The absent player having been recalled, at a given signal everyone shouts simultaneously his or her own word, by which means the proverb must be guessed.

BALL.

THE game of ball is of very ancient origin, and there are many ways of amusing oneself with it. The players may stand in a ring a fair distance apart, and throw the ball from one to the other. Those who miss have to remain in the attitude in which they were when they dropped the ball. At the end of the game the circle presents a very grotesque appearance. Another way is, that whoever misses goes out of the game, so the circle diminishes till only two remain; these continue till one fails and leaves the other the winner. A more exciting way is for the players to take the names of the days of the week, or if more than seven the months of the year. Then, for instance, Monday says; "The ball falls to Thursday." Thursday catches it and says: "The ball falls to Tuesday," and so on. Whoever misses pays a forfeit. Throwing the ball to the ground and letting it bound before catching it, or making it bound against a wall, are other varieties of the game.

SHADOW BUFF.

A SMALL sheet or table cloth must be fastened up at one end of the room. "Buff" sits facing it. A light is placed on a table a short distance behind "Buff," all the others in the room being extinguished. The players then pass in succession between "Buff" and the light, distorting their features and performing various odd antics, in order to make their shadows entirely different to their ordinary appearance. "Buff" must then guess whose shadow it is, when he guesses correctly that player takes his place.

THIS AND THAT.

THIS game is rather a catch, only two of the company should know it. As one leaves the room, her accomplice whispers the word *that;* then those in the room fix on an object which one touches, for instance, basket. The absent one is then called in and asked: "Is it this paper knife?" "This rose?" "This book?" "*That* basket?" "Yes!"

BUZ.

THIS is a very old game. All the players sit in a circle and begin to count in turn, but when the number 7, or any multiple of 7 comes, they say "buz" instead. If anyone forgets this, he is put out and the game commences over again. "Fiz" for five makes a variety.

FAMILY COACH.

THE more there are to play at this game the better. All the players take the name of something relating to a coach, such as the whip, right-front wheel, old lady, postilion, luggage, etc. One of the players has to make up a tale bringing in these various words. As each one's name is mentioned, he should rise and turn round, and when family coach is spoken of, all rise and turn round.

MARY'S GONE A-MILKING.

ALL the children stand in a row, with joined hands, except one, who stands in front of them, and is Mother. They advance and retreat, singing :—

"MARY'S gone a-milking, a-milking,
a-milking;
Mary's gone a-milking, dearest
mother of mine!"

MARY'S GONE A-MILKING—continued.

To which the Mother replies (advancing and retreating):—

> TAKE your pails and go after her, after her, after her;
> Take your pails and go after her, dearest daughters of mine!"

CHILDREN. "Buy me a new pair of milking pails, milking pails, milking pails;
Buy me a new pair of milking pails, dearest mother of mine!"

MOTHER. "What's your father to sleep in, sleep in, sleep in;
What's your father to sleep in, dearest daughters of mine?"

CHILDREN. "Sleep in the washing-tub," &c.

MOTHER. "What am I to wash in?" &c.

CHILDREN. "Wash in a tea-cup," &c.

MOTHER. "A tea-cup won't hold your father's shirt," &c.

CHILDREN. "Wash in a thimble," &c.

MOTHER. "A thimble won't hold the baby's cap," &c.

CHILDREN. "Wash in the river," &c.

MOTHER. "Suppose the clothes should float away," &c.

CHILDREN. "Take a boat and go after them," &c.

MOTHER. "Suppose the boat was to sink with me," &c.

CHILDREN. "Then there'd be an end of you!"

Mother here rushes after the children. If she succeeds in catching one that one must be Mother.

QUEEN ANNE AND HER MAIDS.

ONE child covers her eyes, while the others, standing in a
row close to each other, put their hands
behind them. One has a ball concealed,
which all pretend to have. They then
call the one who has covered
her eyes, and addressing
her sing :—

" QUEEN ANNE, Queen Anne, she
    sits in the sun ;
As fair as a lily, as brown as
    a bun ;
She sends you three letters, and begs you'll read one ! "

To which Queen Anne replies :—

> " I CANNOT read one unless I read all,
> So please Miss Mabel* deliver the ball."

If she has guessed correctly, the one who had the ball takes Queen Anne's place; but if it was a wrong one she hides her eyes again while the ball changes hands.

* Or whatever the name of the one she thinks has it is.

RUTH AND JACOB.

ONE player is blindfolded, and the rest dance in a circle round him till he points at some one. That person enters the ring, and the blindman calls out "Ruth"; "she" answers "Jacob"; and moving about within the circle so as to elude the blindman, continues to answer "Jacob" as often as the blindman calls out "Ruth." This continues until "Ruth" is caught. "Jacob" must then guess who it is he has caught; if he guesses correctly, "Ruth" takes his place, and the game goes on as before; if wrongly, the same one is "Jacob" again.

SKIPPING.

Two children each hold one end
of a rope, and stand so that in turning it just
touches the ground in the middle. How fast
they turn entirely depends on the skipper. Two
can skip at the same time over the rope if it
is a fairly long one. In skipping singly it is
more graceful to watch if the rope is thrown
backwards over the head rather
than forward under the feet.

GENERAL POST.

ONE person is selected as " postman " and blindfolded, the others all take the names of different places, except one, who is chosen as leader, and has a written list of the places chosen by the players. He then calls out: "The post is going from London to York," or any other names as the case may be. The persons named must then exchange seats, the "postman" trying to catch them as they move. Sometimes "general post" is called out, when all change their seats. Whoever is left out becomes "postman."

WORD MAKING.

THE players must all be provided with paper and pencils. They then choose a long word, say Mediterranean, and each player writes it on his paper. When they have done that, they all take the letter "M" and make out of Mediterranean as many words as they can beginning with this letter. They are allowed two minutes, and then they each read out in succession the words they have made. Whoever has one that none of the others thought of counts one. Then the next letter "e" is taken, and so the game continues till the end of the word, when, whoever has the most marks is the winner.

(63)

THE MAGIC ANSWER.

IN this game it is needful that the player who leaves the room should have an accomplice amongst those who stay behind. After the one who has to guess has left the room, the others fix on a word for her to guess on her return. The *right* word, as previously arranged, is the one which is mentioned after any four-legged thing. For instance the accomplice in the room asks her: "Did we name a book?" "No!" "One of the present company?" "No!" "A pen?" "No!" "A basket?" "No!" "A mouse?" (four legs) "No!" "A tea-pot?" "Yes!"

[THE END]